RUDOLF STEINER (1861–1925) called his spiritual philosophy 'anthroposophy', meaning 'wisdom of the human being'. As a highly developed seer, he based his work on direct knowledge and perception of spiritual dimensions. He initiated a modern and universal 'science of spirit', accessible to anyone willing to exercise clear and unprejudiced thinking.

From his spiritual investigations Steiner provided suggestions for the renewal of many activities, including education (both general and special), agriculture, medicine, economics, architecture, science, philosophy, religion and the arts. Today there are thousands of schools, clinics, farms and other organizations involved in practical work based on his principles. His many published works feature his research into the spiritual nature of the human being, the evolution of the world and humanity, and methods of personal development. Steiner wrote some 30 books and delivered over 6,000 lectures across Europe. In 1924 he founded the General Anthroposophical Society, which today has branches throughout the world.

THE WORK OF THE ANGEL IN OUR ASTRAL BODY

RUDOLF STEINER

Sophia Books

Sophia Books
An imprint of Rudolf Steiner Press
Hillside House, The Square
Forest Row RH18 5ES

www.rudolfsteinerpress.com

Published by Rudolf Steiner Press 2006

First published by Rudolf Steiner Press in 1996 as part of the
collection entitled *Angels*

Originally published in German as part of the volume entitled
Der Tod als Lebenswandlung (volume 182 in the *Rudolf Steiner
Gesamtausgabe* or Collected Works) by Rudolf Steiner Verlag,
Dornach. This authorized translation is published by permission
of the Rudolf Steiner Nachlassverwaltung, Dornach

Translated by Anna Meuss
This translation © Rudolf Steiner Press 1996

A catalogue record for this book is available from the British
Library

ISBN-10: 1 85584 198 3
ISBN-13: 978 185584 198 7

Cover by Andrew Morgan
Typeset by DP Photosetting, Aylesbury, Bucks.
Printed and bound in Great Britain by Cromwell Press Limited,
Trowbridge, Wilts.

Contents

Anthroposophical understanding of the spirit must be a leaven, a real power in life, and not merely a theoretical view of life. It can really only fulfil its mission if we develop the inner powers that allow it to come fully alive in us. Connecting with the anthroposophical conception of the spirit we become custodians, as it were, of quite specific, significant processes in human evolution.

Whatever their view of the world, people are generally convinced that thoughts and ideas have no place in it, except as the contents of their own souls. People who hold such views believe that thoughts and ideas as ideals are only embodied in the world to the extent that a person succeeds in implementing them by his physical actions.

The anthroposophical approach asks us to

accept that thoughts and ideas must also find other ways of coming to realization. Recognition of this essential principle implies that anthroposophists must play their part in watching out for the signs of the times. A great deal is happening all the time in world evolution; and it falls to human beings, particularly those of our own time, to acquire real understanding of the world events in which they are involved.

We know that with individual human beings account must be taken of their stage of development as well as external events around them. Just think, putting it very crudely, that events are now happening around individuals who are 5, 10, 20, 30, 50 or 70 years of age. No one in their senses would expect the same reaction from 5-, 10-, 20-, 50- and 70-year-olds. The way people may be expected to react to their environment can only be determined by taking account of their stage of development. Everyone will admit this to be true in the individual case.

Just as there are definite stages in individual

development, with the nature of our powers and faculties different in childhood, mid-life and old age, so are the powers and faculties humanity has as a whole always changing in the course of evolution.

Failing to take note of the fact that the character of twentieth-century humanity differs from that of humanity in the fifteenth century, let alone before and at the time of the Mystery of Golgotha, is to sleep through the process of world evolution. One of the greatest defects, one of the principal sources of error and confusion in our time, is the failure to take note of this, thinking in terms of abstract generalization of individuals or of humanity, with no need to know that humanity is in a process of evolution.

The question is: How can we gain fuller insight into these things? As you know, we have often spoken of one important phase in human evolution. The Graeco-Latin period of civilization, from the eighth century BC to approximately the fifteenth century, was the period when the intellectual or mind soul evolved.[1] Development of the spiritual soul has been in progress from the fifteenth century, a factor in human evolution that concerns our own time in particular. We know that the paramount factor in human evolution from the fifteenth century to the beginning of the fourth millennium is the spiritual soul.

In a true science of the spirit we must never stop at generalizations and abstractions. Always and in all places we must endeavour to grasp the real situation. Abstractions will at most satisfy our curiosity in the ordinary sense of the word. To make the science of the spirit the leaven and essential power in our life we must be profoundly serious rather than curious, and not stop at such abstractions. It is both true and important that living in the age of the spiritual soul we must take special account of its development; but we must not stop there.

To gain a clear conception of these things we must above all consider the nature of man himself in greater detail. In terms of the science of the spirit, the aspects of the human being, from above down, are ego, astral body, ether body—which I have more recently also called the body of generative forces—and physical body. The ego is the only one of these in which we live and function in soul and spirit. It has been given to us through Earth evolution and the Spirits of Form who direct it.[2] Essentially everything that enters into conscious awareness does so through the ego. If the ego did not evolve in a way that allows it to remain connected with the outside world—even just indirectly, through the astral, ether and physical bodies—we would have as little conscious awareness as we have during sleep. It is the ego which connects us with our environment; the astral body is the legacy of the Old Moon evolution that preceded Earth evolution, the ether body of Old Sun evolution, the physical body, in its first rudiments, of Old Saturn evolution.

If you study the description of these bodies in *Occult Science—An Outline*, you will perceive the complex nature of the process in which this fourfold constitution of man came into being. The facts presented in the book clearly show that all the hierarchies were involved in the creation of the astral, etheric and physical bodies, and we can see that these enveloping forms are highly complex by nature. The hierarchies have not only been involved in their creation—they are still active in them. People who think the human being to be merely a combination of bones, blood, flesh, and so on, which is the view held in modern science, physiology, biology or anatomy, do not understand his true nature.

If we consider the reality of these aspects of the human being, perceiving the truth of them, we realize that spirits of the hierarchies are working together in everything that goes on in those bodies without our being conscious of it. From the brief outline of the concerted actions of individual spirits from the hierarchies I have given in *Occult Science—An Outline* you can see how intricate the details must be. Nevertheless, if we want to understand the human being we must go into this further.

It is extremely difficult to consider a specific issue in this field. The situation is highly complex. Suppose someone were to ask: What is the hierarchy of the Seraphim or of the Dynamis doing in the human ether body at the present time in human evolution, in the year 1918? We may ask this just as we may ask whether it happens to be raining in Lugano. Neither question can be answered by merely reflecting or theorizing on it, only by ascertaining the facts. We might send a telegram or a letter, for instance, to find out if it is raining in Lugano. And we must also enter into the facts of the situation if we want to know, say, what is the mission of the Spirits of Wisdom or of the Thrones as far as the human ether body is concerned at the present time. This, however, is an extremely complex issue, and we will never be able to do more than get a bit closer to the areas where such questions arise. Good care is taken that we shall not soar too far aloft and become arrogant and supercilious in our search for knowledge.

The spirits we can see most clearly may be said to be those nearest to us, the ones that directly concern us. And it is important that we see them clearly if we are not to remain asleep at our stations in human evolution.

I am therefore going to speak of something that is less vague and indefinite than the question as to what the Dynamis or Thrones are doing in the human etheric body. A question of immediate concern to people today is what the Angels, the spirits nearest to humanity, are doing in the human astral body at the present time.

The astral body is closest to the ego, so that finding an answer to this question would be of real concern to us. The Angels are the hierarchy immediately above the human hierarchy. We shall ask the modest question as to what the Angels are doing in the human astral body at the present time, a stage in the life of humanity that started in the fifteenth century and will continue to the beginning of the fourth millennium, and we shall find the answer to be really important to us.

What can actually be said when it comes to answering a question such as this? Only that spiritual investigation pursued in all seriousness is not a matter of juggling with ideas or words, but truly takes us into regions where the world of the spirit can be perceived, which is in the regions nearest to us. A truly useful answer can only be found now, in the age of the spiritual soul.

You might think that if this question could have been asked in other times an answer may well have been forthcoming. But it could not have been answered in the age of atavistic clairvoyance nor in the period of Graeco-Latin civilization because the images arising in the mind's eye from atavistic clairvoyance would have obscured anything perceived of the Angel's activities in the astral body. Nothing could be seen of them precisely because human beings had the images that came from atavistic clairvoyance.

In Graeco-Latin times people did not have the thinking power they have today. Our thinking power has increased, especially with the evolution of modern science, and in the age of the spiritual soul such a question can be the subject of deliberate study. The fruits which the science of the spirit can have in life must be evident from the fact that we do not just dole out theories but know how to say things of incisive significance for life.

What are the Angels doing in our astral body? We can discover this if we progress to a level of clairvoyant observation that enables us to see what happens in the astral body. We have to achieve a certain level at least of perception in images if we are to answer the question.

We then find that the spirits from the hierarchy of the Angels—and in a way this means each individual Angel who has a mission relating to every individual human being and also their concerted actions—shape images in the human astral body under the guidance of the Spirits of

Form. We have to reach the level of perception in images before we can know that images are being shaped all the time in our astral body. They arise and pass away, but without them mankind would not evolve according to the intentions of the Spirits of Form. Initially the Spirits of Form are obliged to develop images of what they want to achieve with us during Earth evolution. Later these images become reality in a humanity transformed.

Today the Spirits of Form are creating images in us through the Angels. These images can be perceived with thinking developed to become clairvoyant. We then find that the images are created according to quite definite impulses and principles. Forces for the future evolution of humanity lie in the way these images are created. If we watch the Angels at their work—this may sound strange but that is how it has to be put— we find they have a very definite plan for the future configuration of social life on earth; their aim is to create images in human astral bodies that will bring about definite conditions in the social life of the future.

People may shy away from the notion that Angels want to call forth ideals for the future in them, but that is how it is. The process follows a specific principle, which is that in time to come no human being shall find peace in the enjoyment of happiness if others around him are unhappy. An impulse of absolute brotherliness, making all of humanity one, will govern social life. This principle of brotherliness regarding social conditions in physical life will have to be thoroughly understood.

This is one principle according to which the Angels create images in the human astral body.

There is also another impulse. They have specific objectives not only with regard to outer social life but also for the inner life. Here the aim they pursue with the images imprinted in the astral body is that in future every human being shall see a hidden divine principle in every other human being.

Mark you well, the intention underlying the work of the Angels is that things shall change. In future we shall not consider human beings to be higher animals, considering their physical qualities in both theory and practice. Instead we are to meet every other human being with the full realization that something of the divine foundations of the world is revealing itself in flesh and blood. To conceive man as an image revealed out of the world of the spirit, and do so in profound seriousness, with all our strength—that is the impulse the Angels lay into the images.

Once this is brought to realization there will be a definite consequence. All independent religious feeling developing in humanity in time to come will depend on the individual being recognized in the image of God in real, practical terms and not mere theory. There will then be no need for religious compulsion, for every encounter between individuals will be a religious act, a sacrament, and there will be no more need for a church with physical buildings and institutions to maintain religious life. The church, if it understands itself rightly, must consider it to be its sole aim to render itself superfluous on the physical plane as the whole of life becomes an expression of the realm that lies beyond the senses. Such, at least, is the reason behind the work of the Angels—to bestow complete religious freedom on humanity.

A third objective is to enable human beings to reach the spirit through thinking, crossing the abyss and experiencing the reality of the spirit in their thinking.

Science of the spirit for mind and spirit, religious freedom for the soul, brotherliness for our bodies—this is like cosmic music resounding through the work which the Angels do in the human astral body. All we have to do is raise our consciousness to a different level and we shall feel ourselves transported to this wonderful place of work which the Angels have in the human astral body.

We are in the age of the spiritual soul, when

the Angels do the work I have just described in the human astral body. Humanity must gradually come to be fully conscious of this. It is part of human evolution.

How is it possible to say the kind of thing I have just been saying? Where are we to look for this work of the Angels? Today we still find it in human sleep states, including states of waking sleep. I have often said that even when they are awake people actually sleep through the most important concerns in life. And I can assure you, though you may not be pleased to hear it, that anyone who goes through life with a wide-awake mind will find numbers and numbers of people who are really asleep. They let events happen without taking the slightest interest in them, without troubling their heads over them or connecting with them in any way. Great world events often pass people by just as something happening in the city passes by someone who is asleep; yet those people are ostensibly awake. When people are thus sleeping through some momentous event it can be seen that the Angels are doing their important work in their astral bodies—quite independently of what these people do or do not want to know.

Such things often happen in a way which must necessarily seem highly enigmatic and distinctly odd. We may think some people completely unworthy of entering into any connection with the world of the spirit. But the truth may well be that in this incarnation the person is an absolute dormouse who sleeps through everything that goes on around him. And in his astral body a spirit from the community of Angels is working on the future of mankind. Observation of this astral body shows that it is being used in spite of those conditions.

What really matters, however, is that human beings grow conscious of these things. The spiritual soul must rise to the level where it is able to recognize what can only be discovered in this particular way.

You will now have sufficient background to

understand me when I say that this age of the spiritual soul is moving towards a specific event. Because it involves the spiritual soul you will understand that the effect this event has on human evolution will depend on human beings themselves. This may be a century earlier or a century later, but it is bound to be part of the evolutionary process. It can be characterized by saying that purely out of the spiritual soul, purely out of conscious thinking, human beings must reach the point of actually perceiving what the Angels are doing to prepare the future of humanity. The things we learn through the science of the spirit must become practical wisdom in the life of humanity—so practical that people will be convinced it is part of their own wisdom to recognize the aims of the Angels as I have described them.

The progress of the human race towards freedom has already reached a point where it will depend on human beings themselves whether they are going to sleep through this event or face it in wide-awake consciousness. To meet it in full consciousness would mean this: We can study the science of the spirit. Indeed nothing else is really necessary. It also helps to meditate and use the guidance given in *Knowledge of the Higher Worlds*.[3] But the essential step has already been taken if the science of the spirit has been studied and really consciously understood. Today it can be studied without developing clairvoyant faculties.

Everyone can do so who does not bar his own way with his prejudices. And if people study the science of the spirit more and more thoroughly, assimilating its concepts and ideas, their conscious mind will become so alert that they will be fully aware of events and no longer sleep through them.

We can characterize these events in greater detail. Essentially knowing what the Angel is doing is only a preparation. The important point is that three things will happen at a particular point in time. As I said, depending on how people respond, the time may be earlier or later, or, at worst, they may not happen at all. But the intention is that humanity will be shown three things by the angelic world.

Firstly, it will be shown that their own genuine interest will enable people to understand the deeper side of human nature. A time will come—and it must not pass unnoticed—when human beings will receive an impulse from the world of the spirit through the Angel. This will kindle a far deeper interest in every human individual than we are inclined to have today. Enhanced interest in other human beings will not be of the subjective kind we like to develop at our leisure, but there will be a sudden impetus and a secret will be instilled into us from the realm of the spirit, the secret of what the other person really is. This is something quite real and specific, not any kind of theoretical consideration. People will learn something and this will kindle their interest in every human being. This is the one event, and it will particularly affect the social sphere.

The second event will be that the Angel irrefutably shows the human being that apart from all else the Christ impulse means complete religious freedom for humanity and that the only true Christianity is one that makes absolute religious freedom possible.

The third event will be that we gain irrefutable insight into the spiritual nature of the world.

As I have said, the three events should take place in such a way that the spiritual soul in us participates in it. This is something that will happen in human evolution, with the Angels now working to this end through the images they create in the human astral body.

Let it be emphasized, however, that this impending triple event is subject to man's free will. Many things that should lead to conscious awareness of the event may be and indeed are being left undone.

As you know, other spirits involved in world evolution have an interest in deflecting mankind from its proper course. These are the ahrimanic and luciferic spirits.[4] The events I have just described are part of the divine evolution of man. If people were to follow the dictates of their own true nature they could not really fail to perceive what the Angels are doing in their astral body. But luciferic spirits seek to divert human beings concerning insight into the work of the Angels. They do this by curbing free will. They try to cloud our understanding of the exercise of our free will. True, they desire to make us good— from the point of view from which I am now speaking Lucifer desires goodness, spirituality, for mankind, but he wants to make us into automatons, with no free will. Human beings are to be made clairvoyant according to perfectly good principles, but in an automatic way; the luciferic spirits want to deprive human beings of their free will, the possibility of doing evil.

This has to do with specific secrets of evolution. As you know, the luciferic spirits have remained stationary at other levels of evolution and bring something foreign into the normal evolutionary process. They are deeply interested in seizing hold of us and preventing us from gaining free will because they themselves have not achieved it. Free will can be gained only on earth, but the luciferic spirits want to have nothing to do with the earth; they want only Old Saturn, Old Sun and Old Moon evolution and nothing beyond this. In a sense they hate human free will. They act in a highly spiritual but automatic way—this is highly significant—and want to raise human beings to their own spiritual heights, making them spiritual but automatic. On the one hand this would create the danger that, before the spiritual soul is fully functional, human beings become spiritual automatons and sleep through the revelation that is to come, which I have characterized for you.

Ahrimanic spirits are also working against this revelation. They do not seek to make human beings particularly spiritual but to smother their awareness of their own spirituality. They want to teach people that they are really only a perfectly developed animal. Ahriman is in truth the great teacher of materialistic Darwinism. He also teaches all the technological and practical activity in Earth evolution where nothing is considered valid unless it can be perceived by the senses, the desire being to have widespread technology, with people satisfying their needs for food and drink and other things in the same way as animals do, except that it is more sophisticated. To kill and obscure man's awareness that he is an image of the Godhead—this is the aim ahrimanic spirits are seeking to achieve by sophisticated scientific means in our age.

In earlier times it would have been of no avail for the ahrimanic spirits to obscure the truth for human beings by means of theories. The reason was that in Graeco-Latin times, and even more so before then, people still gained images through atavistic clairvoyance and it did not matter what they thought. They had their images which were like windows into the world of the spirit. Anything Ahriman might have taught them concerning their relation to animals would have had no effect on their way of life. Thinking only became a powerful process—powerful in its impotence, we might say—in our fifth post-Atlantean age, from the fifteenth century onwards. Only then did thinking become effective in taking the spiritual soul into the realm of the spirit or, indeed, preventing it from entering into the world of the spirit. Only now do we live in an age when a scientific theory may be deliberately used to deprive us of our divine nature and all experience of divine nature. This is only possible in the age of the spiritual soul. The ahrimanic spirits therefore seek to spread teachings among humanity that obscure man's divine origin.

This reference to the streams that go against normal and divine human evolution may show how we must conduct our lives so that we do not sleep through the revelation that is to come. Otherwise a great danger will arise. We have to be on the alert for this, or something will develop that may be a great and real danger to Earth evolution, taking the place of the significant event intended to play a momentous part in shaping the future evolution of Earth.

Some spiritual beings achieve higher development because human beings develop together with them. The Angels do not develop images in the human astral body as a kind of game but in order to achieve something. As the aim they have to achieve lies within earthly humanity itself, the whole matter would become a game if human beings, having reached the stage of the spiritual soul, were to deliberately ignore it. This would make it all into a game. The Angels would be playing a game in the developing human astral body. It is not a game but a serious business only because it comes to realization in humanity. You will realize, therefore, that the work of the Angels must always be a serious matter. Imagine what would happen behind the scenes of existence if human beings were to stay asleep and so turn the work of the Angels into a game!

What if this were to happen after all? What if earthly humanity were to persist in sleeping through the momentous spiritual revelation that is to come? If humanity were to sleep through the middle part, for instance, the matter relating to religious freedom, if they were to sleep through the repetition of the Mystery of Golgotha on the etheric plane, the reappearance of the etheric Christ,[5] or through other things, the Angels would have to achieve their aim in a different way. If human beings did not, while awake, allow the Angels to achieve their aim in human astral bodies, they would achieve it with the help of the physical and ether bodies that remain in bed during sleep. This is where powers to achieve the aim would be sought. The aim not achievable with human beings who are awake, with souls awake in their ether and physical bodies, will be achieved with the ether and physical bodies as they lie asleep, when human beings who should be awake are outside those bodies with their ego and astral body.

Here lies the great danger for the age of the spiritual soul. It may still happen if human beings are not willing to turn to life in the spirit before the beginning of the third millennium. The third millennium begins in the year 2000, and is therefore only a short way ahead of us. It may still be necessary for the Angels to achieve their aim by means of sleeping human bodies. They would have to withdraw all their work from the astral body and take it into the etheric body to do so. But then the human being would have no part in it. The work would have to be done in the ether body when the human being is not present, for if he were present in the waking state he would obstruct it.

This gives you a general idea. But what would be the outcome if the Angels were obliged to do their work without the participation of human beings, doing it in human ether and physical bodies during sleep?

The inevitable effect on human evolution would be threefold. Firstly, something would be engendered in sleeping human bodies, when the human ego and astral body are outside, which human beings would not discover in freedom but simply find to be there when they wake up in the morning. Danger would threaten from certain instinctive perceptions connected with the mystery of birth and conception and with sexual life as a whole that are intended to be part of human nature. The danger would come from certain Angels who themselves would undergo a change, which is something I cannot speak about, for it belongs to the higher secrets of initiation which may not yet be disclosed. But this much can certainly be said: The effect on human evolution would be that certain instincts belonging to the sexual life and to sexual nature would not come to clear conscious awareness in a useful way but become harmful. These instincts would not be mere aberrations but would enter into the social life, configuring it. Something would enter into people's blood as a consequence of sexual life that would above all make people go against brotherliness on earth rather than develop brotherliness. This would be a matter of instinct.

A crucial time will come when the path to the right may be taken—which demands wakefulness—or the path to the left, where people sleep. Instincts of a truly horrific nature would then develop.

What do you suppose scientific experts will say when such instincts emerge? They will consider them a natural and inevitable development in human evolution. Light cannot be shed on such matters by ordinary science, for scientific reasoning can be used to explain why people become angels or devils. In either case one thing always follows from another—the great wisdom of causality! Scientists will be completely blind to the event of which I have spoken, for they will simply consider it to be a natural necessity that people turn into half devils because of their sexual instincts. There can be no scientific explanation, for anything and everything can always be explained in science. The fact is that such things can only be understood by spiritual insight that goes beyond the sphere of the senses.

Secondly, this work, which also brings changes for the Angels, will cause humanity to gain instinctive knowledge of some medicines and harmful knowledge of others. Everything connected with medicine will make great advances in the materialistic sense. People will gain instinctive insight into the medicinal properties of some substances and techniques and this will cause tremendous damage but would be said to be beneficial. Pathological changes will be called normal, for people will find that this leads to a certain technique that pleases them. They will actually like things that in a certain way take humanity into an unhealthy state. Knowledge of the medicinal powers of certain processes and techniques will increase but this will lead into very harmful channels. Out of certain instincts people will know the kind of diseases which can be produced by specific substances and techniques, and they will be able to arrange matters entirely to suit their egotistical purposes, to provoke diseases or not to provoke them.

Thirdly, humanity will get to know specific powers which enable them to unleash tremendous mechanical forces in the world by means of quite simple manipulations—bringing certain wave-lengths into accord. They will instinctively come to realize that it is possible to exercise some degree of mental control over mechanics. This will take the whole of technology along disastrous channels, a state of affairs, however, that will serve human egotism extremely well and please people.

Here we gain clear insight into the evolution of existence, and we perceive a conception of life that can really only be properly appreciated by those who understand that we shall never be clear about these things if we take an unspiritual view of life. People with an unspiritual view of life would not be able to perceive that an approach to medicine was causing harm to humanity, that sexual instincts were going desperately astray, that a terrible hustle and bustle of purely mechanistic activity was arising as forces of nature were utilized through powers of the mind. They would not realize that this meant deviation from the true path, just as someone who is asleep cannot see the thief who comes to rob him; the incident would pass him by; at most he would realize what had happened later, after he had woken up. But it would be a terrible awakening for humanity. People would delight in the instinctive broadening of their knowledge of certain processes and substances; they would gain a certain satisfaction in the pursuit of sexual aberrations, regarding them as evidence of an advanced development of more than human qualities, lack of prejudice and broad-mindedness. In some respects ugliness would be considered beauty and beauty ugliness. None of this would be noticed for it would be taken for natural necessity. It would, however, be a deviation from the path laid down for humanity in the individual nature given to human beings.[6]

I think if we develop a feeling for the way the science of the spirit enters into our attitudes of mind we can also be truly serious in our approach to truths like those presented today, and gain from them what really should be gained from the whole of this science: to recognize a certain obligation, certain responsibilities in life. Whatever our role in life and in the world, it is important that we have the thought: Everything we do must be imbued with and illumined by anthroposophical awareness. We then contribute something to the true advancement of human evolution.

It would be entirely wrong to believe that the true science of the spirit, approached in a serious and worthy mood, could ever divert us from the necessary practical involvement in life. The true science of the spirit makes us wake up with regard to such matters as I have spoken of today.

You may, of course, ask if waking life is harmful to sleep. If we take the analogy that insight into the world of the spirit means to waken at a higher level than we do when we wake from sleep, we may also ask the question, in order to understand the analogy: Can this kind of waking life ever be harmful to sleep? Yes, if it is not what it ought to be! If people spend their waking life as it should be spent, they will also sleep soundly; if they doze through their waking hours, or are lazy, taking the easy way, their sleep will not be sound. The same holds true for the waking life we acquire by working with the science of the spirit. If the science of the spirit helps us to establish a proper relationship to the world of the spirit, this will also guide our interest in the familiar, sense-perceptible aspects of life along the right channels, just as a proper waking life gives sound sleep.

Looking at life in our time we must indeed be asleep if we fail to notice a number of things. Think how people have preened themselves on their conduct of life, particularly in the last few decades! They have finally reached a point where leading positions are held everywhere by people who are utterly contemptuous of the life of ideas, of the spirit. People have gone on to hold forth about their life style, for so far humanity has not been dragged into the abyss. Now, however, some begin to croak, albeit most of them instinctively: A new age must come, all kinds of new ideals must arise! But they are croaking. If these things were to come instinctively, without consciously making the science of the spirit one's own, they would lead to a decline of what should be experienced in the waking state and not to any kind of wholesome transition in evolution.

Anyone who today makes impassioned speeches to people in words they have long been accustomed to hear can usually still count on some applause. But people will have to get used to listening to different words, different ways of putting things, if a social cosmos is to arise from the chaos.

If human beings fail to wake up in a particular era and fail to discover what needs to be done, nothing real will happen. Instead, the spectre of the preceding era will arise. Thus spectres of the past are to be found in many religious communities today, and the spectre of ancient Rome still haunts the sphere of jurisprudence. The science of the spirit exists to make people free in this respect in the age of the spiritual soul, truly guiding them to observe a spiritual fact: What is the work of the Angels in our astral bodies? To talk about Angels and so on in an abstract way can at most be a beginning. Progress requires that we speak in real terms, that is, find the answer to the most immediate question in our present age. This concerns us because the Angel is creating images in our astral body, images that are to configure us for the future, a configuration to be achieved by the spiritual soul.

Without a spiritual soul there would be no need to exert ourselves. Other spirits, other hierarchies, would step in and bring the images created by the Angels to fulfilment. We are, however, intended to develop a spiritual soul, and because of this no other spirits come to bring the work of the Angels to fruition.

Angels were, of course, also at work in the Egyptian era. But other spirits soon came in, and as a result man's atavistic clairvoyance became obscured. Seeing this in their atavistic clairvoyance, human beings wove a dark veil to cover the work of the Angels. Now, however, human beings must remove the veil. They should not sleep through what is being brought into conscious life in an age that will reach its conclusion before the third millennium. Let us draw not only teachings but also resolves from the science of the spirit extended by anthroposophy! Such resolves will give us the strength to be vigilant and alert.[7]

We can get into the habit of being alert. We can pay heed to many things. We can make a start now and find that basically not a day passes without a miracle happening in our life. We can also put this the other way round and say: If we do not discover a miracle in our life on a parti-

cular day, we have merely lost sight of it. Try to
look back on your life in the evening; you will
find some event—small, middling or great—of
which you will be able to say that it came into
your life and took effect in a remarkable way.
You can achieve this if you take a wide enough
view, considering the circumstances and con-
nections in life on a sufficiently wide scale. But
we do not usually do this in ordinary life, because
we do not normally ask ourselves what has been
prevented from happening in some way, for
example.

We do not usually trouble about things that
have been prevented, though if they had happened they would have brought a fundamental
change in our lives. Behind the things which have
been kept out of our lives in some way or other
lies a great deal of what makes us into alert
human beings. What might have happened to me
today? If I ask myself this question every night
and then consider individual occurrences that
might have had one consequence or another,

reflections on life will arise in connection with these questions that bring the element of vigilance into my self-discipline. Thus a start can be made, and it will take us further and further, until finally we explore not only what it means in our life that we intended to go out at half past ten in the morning, for example, but someone turned up at the last minute and stopped us. It annoys us that we were stopped, but we do not ask what might have happened if we really had gone out at the intended time. We do not consider what change there has been.

I have spoken of these things in greater detail here on an earlier occasion. A straight and certain path leads from observation of negative aspects in our lives, which may bear witness to wise guidance, to observation of the Angel who is actively working in our astral body. It is a path that is open to us.

Notes

The text is a record of a lecture Rudolf Steiner gave to members of the Anthroposophical Society in Zurich on 9 October 1918.

GA = *Gesamtausgabe*: the Collected Works of Rudolf Steiner in the original German.

1. For information on the various spiritual bodies Steiner refers to, see *Theosophy* (GA 9), Rudolf Steiner Press 1973.
2. See further in *Occult Science—An Outline* (GA 13), Rudolf Steiner Press 1979.
3. *Knowledge of the Higher Worlds* (GA 10), Rudolf Steiner Press 1969.
4. See further in *The Influences of Lucifer and Ahriman* (various GAs), Anthroposophic Press 1993.
5. See further in *The Reappearance of Christ in the Etheric* (various GAs), SteinerBooks 2003.

6. Rudolf Steiner rarely made predictions connected to specific time-scales. In this case he links the three potentially negative phenomena he describes to 'the year 2000'—although such consequences would only occur if, before that date, 'human beings are not willing to turn to the life of the spirit'.

   This is the first time this lecture is being republished in English since the turn of the millennium, so it would seem apt to refer to Steiner's dramatic comments here. However, whether humanity failed to 'turn to the life of the spirit' before the year 2000, and whether we are now facing the consequences of not doing so (consequences which Steiner summarizes as: 'an approach to medicine ... causing harm to humanity'; 'sexual instincts ... going desperately astray'; and 'purely mechanistic activity ... arising as forces of nature [are] utilized through powers of the mind') is something that each reader will have to decide for him or herself.

7. The above paragraph does not entirely make sense, and it seems that sentences or important parts of sentences may have been omitted from the record.

The meaning may be perceived by comparing it with the statements made earlier in this lecture and in *Spiritual Guidance of the Individual and Humanity* (GA 15), Anthroposophic Press 1994.

Further Reading

Rudolf Steiner's fundamental books:

Knowledge of the Higher Words
also published as: *How to Know Higher Worlds*

Occult Science
also published as: *An Outline of Esoteric Science*

Theosophy

The Philosophy of Freedom
also published as:
Intuitive Thinking as a Spiritual Path

Some relevant volumes of Rudolf Steiner's lectures:

Angels
Evil
Guardian Angels
Guidance in Esoteric Training
Rosicrucian Wisdom

For all titles contact Rudolf Steiner Press (UK) or
SteinerBooks (USA):
www.rudolfsteinerpress.com www.steinerbooks.org

Publisher's Note on
Rudolf Steiner's Lectures

The lectures and addresses contained in this volume have been translated from the German, which is based on stenographic and other recorded texts that were in most cases never seen or revised by the lecturer. Hence, due to human errors in hearing and transcription, they may contain mistakes and faulty passages. Every effort has been made to ensure that this is not the case. Some of the lectures were given to audiences more familiar with anthroposophy; these are the so-called 'private' or 'members' lectures. Other lectures, like the written works, were intended for the general public. The difference between these, as Rudolf Steiner indicates in his *Autobiography*, is twofold. On the one hand, the members' lectures take for granted a background in and commitment to anthroposophy; in the public lectures this was not the case. At the same time, the members' lectures address the concerns and dilemmas of the members, while the public work speaks directly out of

Steiner's own understanding of universal needs. Nevertheless, as Rudolf Steiner stresses: 'Nothing was ever said that was not solely the result of my direct experience of the growing content of anthroposophy. There was never any question of concessions to the prejudices and preferences of the members. Whoever reads these privately printed lectures can take them to represent anthroposophy in the fullest sense. Thus it was possible without hesitation—when the complaints in this direction became too persistent—to depart from the custom of circulating this material "For members only". But it must be borne in mind that faulty passages do occur in these reports not revised by myself.' Earlier in the same chapter, he states: 'Had I been able to correct them [*the private lectures*], the restriction *for members only* would have been unnecessary from the beginning.'

The original German editions on which this text is based were published by Rudolf Steiner Verlag, Dornach, Switzerland in the collected edition (*Gesamtausgabe*, 'GA') of Rudolf Steiner's work. All publications are edited by the Rudolf Steiner Nachlassverwaltung (estate), which wholly owns both Rudolf Steiner Verlag and the Rudolf Steiner Archive. The organization relies solely on donations to continue its activity.

Other budget-priced volumes from Rudolf Steiner Press

Single lectures:
How Can I Find the Christ?
The Dead Are With Us

Meditations:
Calendar of the Soul, The Year Participated
The Foundation Stone Meditation